Contents

What is a habitat?

A **habitat** is a place where plants and animals can find what they need to live. Just like you, they need food, water, and shelter.

short-toed eagle

HORRIBLE HABITATS
Rubbish Bins and Landfills

Sharon Katz Cooper

www.raintreepublishers.co.uk
Visit our website to find out
more information about
Raintree books.

To order:
☎ Phone 0845 6044371
🖷 Fax +44 (0) 1865 312263
🖳 Email myorders@raintreepublishers.co.uk

Customers from outside the UK please telephone +44 1865 312262

Raintree is an imprint of Capstone Global Library Limited,
a company incorporated in England and Wales having
its registered office at 7 Pilgrim Street, London, EC4V 6LB
– Registered company number: 6695582

Edited by Charlotte Guillain, Rebecca Rissman,
  and Siân Smith
Designed by Joanna Hinton-Malivoire
Picture research by Tracy Cummins and Heather Mauldin
Originated by Chroma Graphics (Overseas) Pte. Ltd
Printed and bound in China by Leo Paper Products

ISBN 978 1 406212 92 1 (hardback)
14 13 12 11 10
10 9 8 7 6 5 4 3 2 1

ISBN 978 1 406213 00 3 (paperback)
14 13 12 11 10
10 9 8 7 6 5 4 3 2 1

British Library Cataloguing in Publication Data
Katz Cooper, Sharon.
Rubbish bins and landfills. -- (Horrible habitats)
577.5'6-dc22
A full catalogue record for this book is available from the
British Library.

Acknowledgements
The author and publisher are grateful to the following
for permission to reproduce copyright material: Alamy
pp. 4 (© Wildlife/ GmbH), 9 (© Vince Bevan), 10
(© Tim Gander), 17 (© Manor Photography), 18
(© NatureOnline); Peter Arnold Inc.p. 25 (© Heike
Fischer); Bugwood.org p. 20 (© Joseph Berger); FLPA
p. 11 (© Phil McLean); Getty Images pp. 8 (© Jason
Hawkes), 21 (© Emanuele Biggi); David Liebman p. 26;
Minden p. 13 (© Warwick Sloss); National Geographic
Stock p. 19 (© Minden Pictures/Heidi and Hans-Jurgen
Koch); Photolibrary pp. 6 (© Phil McLeanKeith Black), 7
(© Phil McLeanCreatas), 12 (© age fotostock/EA. Janes),
22 (© Satoshi Kuribayashi), 23 (© Werle Werle), 29
(© Oxford Scientific/Geoff Kidd); Photoshot p. 14
(© Bruce Coleman/Len Rue Jr.); Shutterstock pp. 5
(© Elena Elisseeva), 15 (© Mishella), 16 (© PerWil);
Visuals Unlimited, Inc. pp. 24, 27 (© Nigel Cattlin).

Cover photograph of gulls and earthmover reproduced
with permission of Getty Images (© Stephen Wilkes).

Every effort has been made to contact copyright holders
of material reproduced in this book. Any omissions will
be rectified in subsequent printings if notice is given to
the publishers.

Some words are shown in bold, **like this**. You can find
out what they mean by looking in the glossary.

5

Lakes, fields, and forests are **habitats**. Some surprising places are habitats, too. You can even find plants and animals living where we put our rubbish.

A **landfill** is a place where rubbish collectors bring rubbish from houses and cities. The workers at a landfill bury rubbish between layers of soil.

Landfills can be huge!

8

landfill

9

Squawking seagulls

You may see hundreds of seagulls swooping around a **landfill**. Seagulls eat rotting food from landfills. They also take some of this tasty food back to their chicks nearby.

FUN FACT

Seagulls feed their chicks by vomiting food into their tiny beaks.

11

Rats everywhere!

Rats are the most famous rubbish bin and **landfill** animals. Rats can find many tasty scraps of food there. They feed on the newest rubbish to arrive before it gets buried.

FUN FACT

Rats can't vomit.
They also can't burp.

hawk

Hawks fly around **landfills** to hunt for rats. The hawks swoop down from the sky. They use their **talons**, or claws, to catch a rat. Once the rat is dead, they pick it apart and eat it with their sharp beaks.

dead rat

Watch out for pigeons

Pigeons are found around rubbish piles. They eat everything they can find there. Pigeons can spread dirt. Some illnesses or **diseases** can be caused by pigeon poo.

How many pigeons can you see here?

16

Here come the flies!

Flies like rubbish because of all the rotting food there. Flies land on a piece of food. They vomit on it to help break it down into smaller pieces. Then they slurp it up.

fly

FUN FACT

Some flies feed on blood rather than rubbish! Stable flies will bite people, pets, and other animals near rubbish bins and drink their blood.

19

Fly eaters

Spiders can also be found around rubbish. They build webs to catch flies and other animals that like to live near the rotting food.

web

spider

When a spider finds a fly, it **injects**, or puts, poison into the fly. The poison makes the fly **paralyzed**, or unable to move. Then the spider can suck out the fly's insides.

Spiders inject poison through pointed teeth called **fangs**.

fangs

yellow sac
spider

FUN FACT

In North America, yellow sac spiders can sometimes be found under rubbish bin lids. If a mother spider stays with her babies while they hatch, they could eat her.

Hungry cockroaches

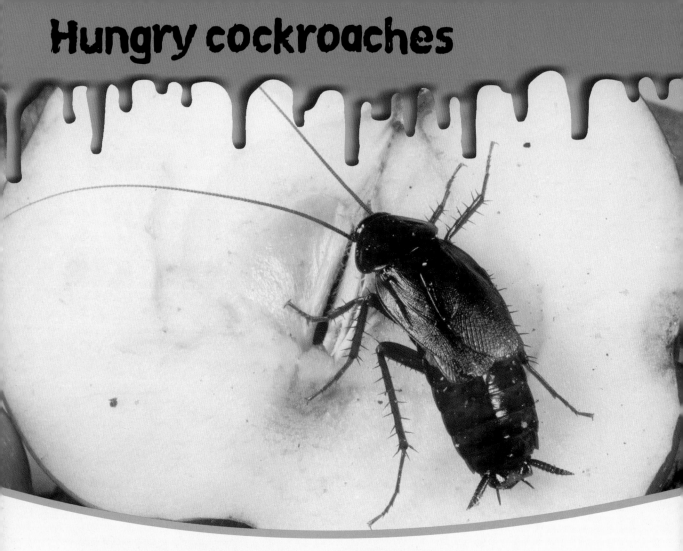

Cockroaches are common around **landfills** and rubbish bins. Rubbish bins are full of rotting food which makes them like a restaurant for cockroaches!

24

FUN FACT

Cockroaches can feel air move behind them with two hairs on their bottoms. That feeling helps them escape quickly from **predators** or things that want to eat them.

25

Cockroaches eat more than rotting food in a rubbish heap. They also like to eat glue from envelopes and stamps. Why? Sometimes glue is made from boiled parts of dead animals!

Cockroaches can live for about a week without their heads!

Rotting food

Many animals like to eat rotting food. Do this experiment to find out how the process of rotting begins. Be sure to talk to an adult about it first!

What you need:
- a piece of stale bread
- water
- a plastic container with a lid

What to do:
1. Use a bit of water to wet your bread. Don't soak it – just get it a little wet.

2. Place your wet bread in the container. Put the lid on loosely. Keep the container in a dark place.

3. Leave it for three days, then look at it, but don't touch it. What do you see?

4. Leave it for another four days and take another look. What do you see? What do you smell?

5. When you have finished the experiment ask an adult to help you to clean the container and lid.

bread

mould

Glossary

disease illness

fangs sharp, pointed teeth

habitat place where animals or plants live and grow

inject to put something into something else

landfill place where rubbish is collected and buried

paralyzed unable to move

predator animal that eats another animal

talons sharp claws on bird feet

Find out more

Find out

How big is the largest cockroach?

Books to read

Bug Books: Cockroach, Karen Hartley, Chris Macro, and Philip Taylor (Heinemann Library, 2008)

Bug Books: Fly, Karen Hartley, Chris Macro, and Philip Taylor (Heinemann Library, 2008)

The Amazing World of Microlife: Microlife that Rots Things, Steve Parker (Raintree, 2006)

Websites

http://www.recyclezone.org.uk/home_az.aspx
This website shows you how to reduce your rubbish by making compost and building your own wormery.

http://yucky.discovery.com/flash/roaches/
Find out interesting facts about cockroaches on this website.

Index